T0194113

The Power of Being Yourself

Navigating the Corporate World
When You Are a Minority

Steven W. Lyle

iUniverse, Inc.
Bloomington

THE POWER OF BEING YOURSELF
NAVIGATING THE CORPORATE WORLD
WHEN YOU ARE A MINORITY

iUniverse books may be ordered through booksellers or by contacting:

iUniverse
1663 Liberty Drive
Bloomington, IN 47403
www.iuniverse.com
1-800-Authors (1-800-288-4677)

Because of the dynamic nature of the Internet, any web addresses or links contained in this book may have changed since publication and may no longer be valid. The views expressed in this work are solely those of the author and do not necessarily reflect the views of the publisher, and the publisher hereby disclaims any responsibility for them.

Any people depicted in stock imagery provided by Thinkstock are models, and such images are being used for illustrative purposes only.

Certain stock imagery © Thinkstock.

ISBN: 978-1-4759-7661-8 (sc)
ISBN: 978-1-4759-7662-5 (hc)
ISBN: 978-1-4759-7663-2 (e)

Library of Congress Control Number: 2013902815

Printed in the United States of America

iUniverse rev. date: 4/25/2013

Table of Contents

Preface

I am a former US Army officer who served three years of active duty and seven years in the Army Reserves. I received a Bronze Star during the Gulf War, and I am a proud father of two sons. I serve as the Chief Diversity Officer and Director of Engineering Workforce Development for Texas Instruments (TI), one of America's giant technology companies. I have been with TI for thirty-three years.

Having started my career at TI as a software programmer analyst, over the years I have had the opportunity to serve in numerous leadership roles, in addition to my present position mentioned above. My past leadership roles have included the Chief Information Technology Officer role for TI's Consumer Products Business; the Director of Quality for TI's Information Technology (IT) Group; the Director of the first IT Management Consulting Practice for TI's Software Business; the Director of Business Excellence for TI's Semiconductor Business; and the Worldwide Staffing Director for the company. I have also had the distinct honor of serving on various university and nonprofit advisory boards, including Texas Tech University, Southern Methodist University, the University of Texas at Dallas, and Catalyst.

From an experience standpoint, the common thread that runs through the thirty-three years that I have enjoyed working with TI is the work that I have done in the area of reengineering business and operational processes, as well as the human side of the resulting changes and transitions.

The common thread that runs through the thirty-three years from a people standpoint (inside of TI and externally) is the caliber of people that I have had the opportunity to work with and learn from. They are some of the brightest minds in world. The diversity of the TI population alone is truly amazing. I found a true passion for helping to ensure that the company's corporate culture allows all those bright minds to do their best work.

My first publication was back in 1997, when I teamed up with Dr. Robert A. Zawacki, a professor emeritus of management and international business at the University of Colorado. That article was entitled "Centers of Excellence: Empowering People to Manage Change" and was published in the winter 1997 issue of *Information Systems Management*. It was a follow-up to an article published in the March 31, 1997, issue of *ComputerWorld*, which described my involvement in helping to restructure the IT organization of TI. At the time, the Centers of Excellence organization model was a way to organize IT organizations so as to maximize the development of the talent.

I value all my past work, but it was not until I stopped hiding my true self—the authentic me, a gay man—that I found personal fulfillment in that work. Although I achieved success early in my career, it was not until I came out of the closet in the workplace that I truly felt successful. It made a world of difference both in how I feel about myself and the personal commitment I have to the people and company, and this is what has helped me do my best work. Regardless of your minority status, you can truly be yourself at work, and in doing so, you will add additional value to your company.

In my journey toward authenticity, I have gained a real sense of the human factors involved in dealing with the majority while being a minority. I would like to share these with you. I believe it can make a positive difference for you in how you feel about yourself, your success on the job, and the contribution you make to your company as a member of a minority group within the company. Even if you are a member of the majority at your company, you can add additional value to the company by increasing your knowledge and awareness of the various minority groups around you.

I grew up in Scottsville, a small town in Kentucky. Scottsville had fewer than 2,500 people at that time. The best thing to do in a town like that is not to be different. I saw what being different got you: I just had to look at the black people in town. They all lived in what was called "Box Town," a place I was told I did not want to go to. There was also the guy who was called the "town queer." People just assumed he was gay. They would laugh and make fun of him. As for the two Asians in town, you would have thought they were aliens. How did these people get here? Why are they here? Will more of them come? Then there were the two "sisters" who lived together. Nice older women. Both were teachers, but people would ask, "Are they *really* sisters?" They looked nothing alike. There were lots of whispers: "Do you think they are … lesbians? God forbid that we would have those types of women teaching our children." It just went on and on.

While I was growing up, it seemed that being different meant too many questions and problems. There seemed to be fear on both sides, from those asking the questions to those providing—or hiding—the answers. Fear held so tight a hold that I learned at an early age to stay hidden, letting only my surface show. The less anyone knew, the better. I lived by the "I hope you don't ask, because I don't want to tell" rule. Emotional distance became my best friend.

I was in the fifth grade when my father passed away. He was an alcoholic. When asked how he died, I would say, "Of a heart attack." That answer garnered sympathetic responses like, "Oh my God, that is so tragic!" Had I said, "He drank himself to death," it would have garnered, "Oh my!" And I would have then become "the son of, you know, that alcoholic."

I also learned that hiding your innermost self was safer. At an early age, I realized I did not feel the same way about girls that other boys did. This was not something I felt I could talk about. I had heard about the "town queer," and I knew I did not want people thinking about me like that.

So life went on, and I chose to hide important defining elements of myself for fear of not being accepted, or worse, being ostracized. As I grew older, my denial became my reality, and I spent a lot of energy being someone I was not, including being the heterosexual male who dates women, meets the "right" one, and marries her. I married my high school sweetheart when I was twenty-two, after graduating from Western Kentucky University in 1979 with a degree in information technology and business. I was hired right out of college by TI. Shortly after starting with the company, I went on military leave of absence (LOA) in order to fulfill my ROTC obligation. After serving three years of active duty, I returned to TI and remained in the active Army Reserves. It was many years later that I was called to active duty and deployed to Saudi Arabia during the Gulf War. After five months in Saudi Arabia, I was awarded the Bronze Star medal. After returning from the war, I continued my career at TI and divorced my wife of ten years. I became a single parent of two sons in their early teens. Although divorce was a big step in becoming who I needed to be, it was just that: a single step. Many more would follow.

Finally, with some trepidation, I attended a Stonewall Business Association meeting in Dallas. Stonewall is a professional business networking organization for gays and lesbians, and I was not fully comfortable being there. While at the meeting, I spoke to a gay couple who were very connected with the business community in Dallas. I mentioned that I worked at TI and had been with the company for fifteen years.

"I wish I could come out at my company," I told them.

They looked at me in surprise. "Steve, don't you know that TI has a fairly active LGBT employee resource group?" they said.

I was stunned. LGBT stands for lesbian, gay, bisexual, and transgender. I had no idea such an employee group existed at TI.

They literally took me by the hand and walked me over to meet the woman who headed the LGBT employee group at TI, and she proceeded to fill me in on the group and how to become involved.

At that moment, I realized just how deep in the closet I was—so much so that I had avoided even knowing what my own company was doing. It was like being in denial. As long as I could believe my company would not be accepting, I was justified in hiding. There was a strange sense of comfort in that, as odd as it might seem.

Over the next several months, I attended a few of the meetings of the LGBT group and met several of the members. I was impressed that they were focusing on making the company more productive and discussing how to increase the contributions of the LGBT employees.

There was open discussion on what was working well and what still needed to be done at the company. I began to see where I could help make a difference. But there was still that barrier: how to come out. I now had a support group of sorts and a growing understanding that I could not help myself or the company unless I started on that journey. And yet the fear remained strong.

It wasn't until my then-boss started asking me questions about my weekends, my family, and my personal life that I realized I could not evade the truth any longer. It wasn't that she was probing for the wrong reasons. She really just wanted to get to know me, as we worked very well together. She saw me holding back; she saw me hiding. It became so awkward not to be straight with her—no pun intended. It reached the point where I had to start fabricating things to keep my truth hidden.

That was when I realized I had to come out; I had to be authentic. I had to take that chance in order for the relationships with my boss grow. Was it easy? No.

I can remember the moment as if it were yesterday. She walked into my office that Monday morning, just as she often did, asking about my weekend. This time, after exchanging pleasantries, I asked her to close the door.

I then opened up and told her about me. I told her a little about my journey in coming out to my sons and the relationship with my partner. I mentioned to her my fear of coming out at work and the concerns that I had. I told her that my desire was to be authentic with her and with others about who I was—who I am—as the relationships I have at work are very important to me. She was very reassuring that my being gay did not make any difference to her, and she felt it would be received in a positive way by other TI leaders as well. From that point on, there was an easiness that I cannot to this day adequately describe. I never believed I could ever be myself at work, or that it would make a difference in my work life. But it did.

For the first time, I felt I could go to work and actually relate to my boss on multiple levels. I could have an authentic relationship with her. I could be totally truthful. When I opened up to her, the level of trust soared, and my ability and desire to go the extra mile increased exponentially. Keep in mind, I had already had a lot of success in my career at TI, but this was different. I now became fully committed to a workplace where I could bring my full being each and every day. I thought to myself, if *I can really be who I am here, I want to invest my discretionary energy into this place.* I felt a freedom I had never before felt in my life. It was a new beginning that would be repeated again and again.

For me, like other LGBT people, as well as those of other minority groups, every new business associate represents another recalibration. Allowing the authentic you to show is not a one-time event. It is a process that is repeated every time new people, new work associates, enter your life. It is about letting the world know who you really are.

It has truly been a journey, and I am grateful to all the people who have been in my life and who are in my life today. Who's to say what might have been different had I confronted the truth earlier in life? It really doesn't matter at this point in time. What does matter is what I do from here on out. Now that I am fifty-five years of age, I can safely say that the relationships I have in my personal and professional life are authentic. Wow, it took a long time!

Acknowledgments

As with any worthwhile endeavor, there are those people who facilitate your efforts—those individuals who help motivate your forward movement and who continue to believe in you.

I have been blessed with such people in my life. Without their encouragement and belief in me, this book would not have happened, and I would have regretted not writing it.

First, I would like to thank Dr. Alvin Granowsky for his years of mentorship to me as a professional and a writer. Harvard educated, Al has written many books over the years, and he was gracious enough to help me focus my thoughts sufficiently to compile the content of this book. Without his insight and feedback, it would have proved to be a much more difficult task.

Second, I have to thank my family. My partner, Daniel Thomas Kamide was a constant force in ensuring that I made progress. He gave me an understanding spirit by allowing me time on weekends to be by myself to form my thoughts. He read through all the rough drafts of the manuscript, offering ever-valuable honest critiques. His love and strength of character inspire me.

My sons, Paul and Brandon, with their focus on making their lives the best they can be, also inspired me to complete this book. They are my pride and joy, and they are men of strong character. Through them I see so much acceptance of diversity. I see so much fullness in their thinking as it relates to making a difference regardless of one's circumstances. They kept reminding me to come through on the completion of this book, and I could not let them down.

Also, I wish to thank my Texas Instruments (TI) colleagues past and present for embracing the spirit of inclusion and innovation and all that comes with it. I have truly felt blessed to work with each and every one of them, and for a company that cares not about *what* you are, but *who* you are and what you bring to the table.

Last, but certainly not least, I thank my heavenly father for his constant watch over me. He has not failed me and has served as my father on earth as well. Without him, I would have nothing.

Introduction

—————◆◆————

As you grow older, you'll find that the only things
you regret are the things you did not do.

—Zachary Scott
Actor

Regardless of who you are—an individual contributor, a manager, part of the majority seeking greater understanding, or a member of the minority as a result of race, nationality, religion, gender, sexual orientation, or whatever—you can turn your unique difference and/ or your increased understanding of diversity and inclusion into an advantage for you, your family, and your company. It is my hope that the ideas presented here will help you increase your knowledge on your journey to greater success.

Over my thirty-three years of experience in the business world, I have observed the efforts people make to fit in, to hide their true selves so as to fit into the group; in the process, they each become a commodity versus a unique product. I was one of those people.

For me, disappearing did not happen from a skills and abilities standpoint. Like everyone else, I wanted to stand out in that arena. It arose from my personal life—from my wanting to hide the authentic me. I rationalized that the less people knew about me personally; the less likely they would be to discuss topics that were not relevant to our business: The fact that I have two sons should mean nothing to my business colleagues. The fact that I love to run should mean nothing if

I know how to "run the numbers." The fact that I am gay is not relevant to my performance in the workplace.

What I have come to realize is that it does matter. Regardless of your difference—race, religion, nationality, gender, sexual orientation, education, age, introversion, or whatever else—what's important is for you to be you and to leverage that difference to the advantage of your organization, your company, and your business interests. You need to be yourself because the authentic you is the valuable you.

Does it sound like a platitude to you—something your mother would say as you go off to your first day of school? "Now, Johnny (or Janie), just be yourself, and everyone will like you." That's not what I'm saying. What I'm saying is more like, "Be proud of who you are and all that you have to offer." My point is that it is important that you take your total self to work, from head to toe, from the inside out: the authentic you.

This book is about taking all the aspects of you, all that makes up the authentic you, to the workplace. It's about bringing a perspective to the table that is different because you are different. It is your unique perspective—unique because it's yours.

I see advantages coming to people willing to bring it all to the table—advantages to them and to the enterprises they are a part of. Moderation and judgment of course always matter, but I submit that this is what companies need and expect people to do, even if the powers that be in a company don't say it, and in some ways, don't show it.

What you typically hear is, "Contribute to the bottom line." Indeed we all must do that to ensure the profitability of the business. However, to do that most effectively, you need to bring a different perspective to the table, which means bringing your thoughts and ideas to the surface. Remember, your ideas, your concepts—your perspective is different because you are different.

If your focus is on blending in—suppressing your personal differences on the job—you risk having and expressing ideas and opinions that are as bland as you are trying to be.

Your life experiences as a minority give you an advantage that will benefit the group. You have life experiences that those in the majority do not have. I believe that most of us in a minority group have ideas, opinions, and suggestions that can provide added dimensions to company decision making, thereby adding a potential premium to the bottom line ... *if only we were heard.*

Marketing people have known it for years. We have all heard about it: "differentiate your product" from others to win in the market. However, when it comes to us as individuals, we typically want to blend in. As minority individuals, we often resist differentiation.

As you move along your journey, you might consider seeking mentors along the way, individuals who can help you navigate and learn. Some of them may even become your sponsors as they begin to understand and see the positive difference that you are making.

Mentorship and Sponsorship

Mentorship and sponsorship have been essential to me in both my personal and professional life. Many people think of these as equivalents. Although they are related, they are very different. *Mentorship* involves helping someone navigate through a section or sections of a journey, providing helpful advice and honest feedback to facilitate improvement. *Sponsorship* is the active involvement in someone's advancement, whether personally or professionally, by being their advocate when it really counts.

I have been fortunate to have individuals who cared enough about me to mentor and/or sponsor me through various stages of my life. Mentoring is very important, but sponsoring is critical. We can often identify mentors in an organization. What we lack sometimes is access to individuals who are willing to sponsor members of a minority group. It's that sponsorship that can mean the difference between success and great success. A sponsor actively looks for ways that the company can leverage the differences and talents of a specific individual.

Mentoring and/or sponsorship are "must-haves" early in any individual's career. It is important to everyone, but more important for a person in a minority group. "Why?" you may ask. I believe it is because it can be very difficult for those in a minority group to convey their life experiences to the majority and achieve a high degree of connection. This is usually because the majority cannot relate those experiences to their own. A mentor or sponsor can help bridge communication and open doors that might not otherwise be opened. Connection is essential in building and sustaining relationships.

It is important to stress that communication and connection are a two-way street. It is not all up to the mentor/sponsor to ensure communication and connection. Nor is it solely the responsibility of the majority to accept the minority person. The minority individual also has to be actively committed to making the most of the mentoring or sponsorship relationship. Being civil, courteous, and professional are essentials for all people, and perhaps even more so for a person in a minority who may be more likely to be judged.

This book offers ideas for individuals, as well as potential mentors and sponsors, to consider as they press forward to improve the workplace and themselves. Each chapter expounds on a specific idea to help individuals navigate the corporate world as persons in a minority. The chapters are organized in the following manner: (1) a brief perspective on a specific tip; (2) a situational challenge with various options and associated probable outcomes; (3) suggestions for self-improvement for the individual and the manager; (4) a concise summary.

Idea #1

Be Comfortable in Your Own Skin—
Breaking the Cycle of Discomfort

The only limit to our realization of tomorrow
will be our doubts of today.

—Franklin Delano Roosevelt
Thirty-Second President of the United States (1933–45)

It's very difficult to do your best work if you are not comfortable in your own skin. You have to be aware of the internal voice that is constantly sending you messages about how to act, what to say, and what you believe others are thinking and saying about you, your work, "people like you."

So what messages are you giving to yourself? Are you telling yourself that your opinion does not have merit in a discussion? Are you telling yourself that no one would understand where you are coming from? That your perspective would be meaningless, even though you think that the proposed approach will be offensive to people from your background?

Are you telling yourself that perhaps you are overreacting and would be considered narrow-minded or an out-of-touch naysayer—that people would think you are not culturally savvy enough to understand the bigger picture?

Do you think that your coworkers harbor ill feelings about your nationality or race, and that they believe you don't deserve the job you have?

The negative messages go on and on. You want to delete the tapes, but it seems that they are burned into your mind.

So you convince yourself that being quiet and letting the plan move forward without your input is the safest bet.

Then, the plan is implemented and is not effective, especially in the minority markets. The company loses market share and revenue. What do you tell yourself? That it would have happened anyway?

This type of scenario plays out every day in corporate America as those of us in the minority wrestle with our inner conflict: Should we speak out when the voice in our head tells us not to?

In some cases, the voice in your head can become a chip on your shoulder. You start believing these negative thoughts to be truths, and they color how you view others. You become hypersensitive and quick to take offense. You strike back at what you perceive to be put-downs, and as a result you alienate a colleague who meant no offense.

Or you may find yourself becoming withdrawn, which causes people to see you as standoffish, so they avoid communicating and spending time with you. This of course feeds your belief that neither you nor your opinion matter to them, and it becomes a downward spiral.

Perhaps you believe that the kudos always go to the white guy. You don't see a black person getting the credit. Or, you don't see a Hispanic or an Asian person for that matter. So you start thinking that the white male has it all: he gets all the credit for having the great ideas. I mean, after all, you had a better idea. But you just knew if you voiced it, you would be shot down.

Perhaps you say to yourself, "No one wants to hear an idea from a woman. It's a man's world."

Perhaps you are an introvert and you say to yourself, "I get so nervous when I speak out. I feel like the group is full of aggressive people all vying for attention. No one will hear my opinion." So you remain silent, and people assume you have nothing of worth to offer. The cycle continues.

Does any of this sound like you? It's not until you reach inside to explore the tapes in your head, the thoughts that hold you back from bringing your whole self to the workplace, that your company can have the opportunity to fully benefit from the insights and life experiences your difference provides. And you can achieve the appreciation and advancement that your difference can mean for your company's bottom line and success.

If you don't find your comfort zone, there is a strong likelihood you will not speak up in the group. No one will hear your opinion. The bottom line is that you will not have the opportunity to make an impact.

The Situation

Now let's look at a situation.

Joe has been with the Bonzo Company for twenty-five-plus years. During that time, he has been instrumental in bringing new concepts from the drawing table to the market. Over the past four years, Joe's work group has dramatically changed. With the influx of new talent, the average age in his work group has dropped by almost fifteen years.

Fitting in had never previously been an issue for Joe. He never really thought about his age at work, as most of the members of his team were about his age, some a little older. But now he is finding it harder to relate to his coworkers, some of whom are young enough to be his son or daughter. This is beginning to negatively affect Joe's approach to his work.

Recently, in a very important project design review, Joe remained silent as the team of younger engineers discussed an approach to a highly technical issue. As Joe listened, he heard them talk about the same approach that he remembered not working in a similar situation some years before.

He wanted to speak up many times during the meeting, yet he remained silent. He thought to himself, "If I say anything, I'll sound like I'm discounting their ideas. I'll come across as a naysayer, a negative old-timer who is not open to new ideas." This fear stopped Joe from offering some potentially important information that the team could have learned from.

The Challenge

The overall challenge is how to integrate multigenerational workers into a cohesive team. The challenge for Joe is to grow more comfortable being the oldest member of the team. He needs to grow secure in the realization that the difference in his age is a positive, providing additional experiences that his younger team members need. The challenge for management is to be aware of the situation and help Joe face his situation head-on.

Options and Probable Outcomes

Option 1: Joe remains silent.

He struggles to manage his fears, but he succumbs to them, feeling that he cannot make a positive difference, so there's no point to even try.

The probable outcome is that the team will struggle to come up with a solid approach, but because of their lack of experience, they will end up going down a path that was taken some years ago and that did not work out well. They will end up losing valuable time in bringing the product to market; or worse, they will spend the time creating an inadequate product design that hurts the company's bottom line.

Option 2: Joe speaks up with a dismissive "been there, done that" approach.

He describes the past failed attempt/approach but offers no insight into what could have been done differently.

The probable outcome is one of a self-fulfilling prophecy. The team may look at him as bringing the team down, as not seeing the "what-ifs" of possibilities and instead focusing on the "done that" negatives. They may tune him out as out-of step, an old man blocking new thinking. As a result, they may end up with the same business design as occurred in option one.

Option 3: Joe speaks up with a positive, solution-oriented attitude.

He describes the past flawed attempt/approach, but also shares the lessons learned and offers ideas of what could have been done differently.

The probable outcome is that the team will get the benefit of not only knowing of the past attempt but also gaining insight into how to avoid the mistakes. They will have the opportunity to take the lessons learned from the past and build them into their own new approach.

In this option, Joe becomes a voice of influence, a link from the past to the present. Thereby, he raises his own value and the value of the team. The product launches and is highly successful.

Self-Improvement Tips

For the Individual

Think about the image you are projecting to your colleagues. Write down on a piece of paper whatever you think that image is. Be honest with yourself. Find someone whom you know to be an honest critic and ask that person to share his or her perception of what you are projecting.

Use the feedback to modify those negative tapes inside your head that keep you from being comfortable in your own skin. See those tapes for what they really are: roadblocks that keep you from contributing to your company's success—and your own.

What Can a Manager Do?

Moving Joe to choose option 3 is key. How can a manager accomplish this?

First, a manager must be in tune with an employee's change in behavior. If you have a person who has gone from speaking out frequently to total silence, you must attempt to understand what has changed.

Of course, with the ever-changing organization structures, it could be that you are new to the group and do not know Joe.

Key here is to make it a point to get to know Joe. Gain knowledge of his past successes and talk to his previous managers and supervisors. Human Resources (HR) is usually a good, unbiased source of history.

You can encourage Joe to speak out by asking him to do so prior to a specific meeting. Let him know that you value his opinion and experience, and that you will be asking him to specifically give some history on a topic and to offer the team tips on how to improve.

This approach helps to draw Joe out because it reinforces to the team that you value experience. If Joe needs to build up his confidence level, you might even consider having him convey his thoughts to you one-on-one, and then you can bring them to the meeting and give the credit to Joe. This helps to boost his confidence, paving the way for him to speak up in future meetings.

The Manager as Sponsor

Regardless of age, if you see what a person can and does contribute, ensure that others do as well. Look for ways to showcase that individual's contributions and knowledge in meetings and other situations that really matter.

Summary of Situation

Leveraging all the talent within yourself and your organization is fundamental to a high-performing team. New ideas come from new and experienced employees alike. All team members should be valued.

Idea #2

Bring Your Total Self to Work— Breaking the Cycle of Invisibility

Being yourself is not remaining what you were, or being satisfied with what you are. It's a point of departure.

—Sydney Harris
Columnist and Author

Bring your total self to work. Now what does that mean?

You may have the tendency to take what is different about you—that which makes your view of life different and your business perspective different—and leave it at the doorstep of your company. Remember, when you hide that difference, you also hide your uniqueness. Your uniqueness makes you, *you.*

My partner and I routinely read the news together on weekend mornings. It is one of our favorite things to do together. As I was reading the World section of the *Dallas Morning News* one day, an article really popped out at me. The title of the article was "In Iraq, living requires lying." Wow! The headline, to me, was so powerful. The article was about how Shiites become Sunnis, and Sunnis portray themselves as Shiites, when looking down the barrel of a gun.

The article was about having to hide who you are in order to survive. What was so interesting to me was that the article was depicting the horror of the situation in Iraq. I thought to myself, *This same situation plays out for those in a minority who feel like they have to hide to survive in the United States.* I started thinking about the countless gay men and women who, just by virtue of who they are, would face a "firing squad" at work if people found out the truth.

When the war in Iraq was just beginning to heat up, I began to receive letters from the US Army and neighboring Army Reserve units asking that I rejoin the active reserves. After the first Gulf War, I went from active to inactive, as I didn't want to have my professional and personal life at risk again. I also knew that if I served again, I would have to serve as an openly gay man.

As the months went by, the letters continued. I began to see the writing on the wall: at some point, I would be requested to report to active reserve duty. After much consideration, I decided that if I was really needed, perhaps I could do it again. After all, we all need to do our part to ensure freedom and safety for our country. However, I knew I would have to serve as an openly gay man.

I sat down and wrote a letter stating that I would serve, but not in the closet, and if that would not be possible, I would resign my commission.

After a few short weeks, I received a confirmation of my commission resignation as an officer of the US Army with not so much as a thank-you for my prior service—service for which I had received the Bronze Star. As you might imagine this type of story plays out across the United States every day.

If each of us had an opportunity to walk in someone else's shoes for just one day—let alone one week or one month—I think we would begin to see the world much differently. We would begin to see the energy a person must muster in order to hide and the internal integrity issues that such an individual has to wrestle with. Although the Iraq example is extreme, it is representative of a "lie to survive" culture that can, and does, exist in societies and corporations.

Oftentimes, because you are suppressing your natural minority attributes, even when they are very visible, you stop short of conveying the reasons for your perspective or your approach to something. In some cases, you might defer to someone else's idea because you don't want to go into the reasons why you think the way you do, as it might reveal more than you're comfortable sharing about your difference.

It's understandable that people who are not part of the majority may want to avoid saying or doing something that can feed the stereotype of their minority group. Is this a "damned if you do, damned if you don't situation"? If you say what you truly feel and why you feel that way, you may wind up supporting a negative stereotype and perhaps receive criticism for doing so. On the other hand, if you don't say what you truly feel and why you feel that way, others will probably accuse you of holding back.

I was once told that when you have an opinion, your IQ goes up seven points. I believe that if you have an opinion and you give the background for that opinion, your IQ goes up even more. I also believe that if you have an opinion and you do not express it, your IQ goes down double digits.

The key is to ensure that you align your style and approach with the company culture. The company culture trumps your personal culture. You may think I'm talking out of both sides of my mouth, but I'm really not. What I am saying is that you have to be aware that there are boundaries that you should not cross. For example, you should not express an opinion that puts another minority on the defensive or that attacks the majority.

Your comments should always be about inclusiveness and building trust among coworkers and others, whether on projects, committees, initiatives, or anything else. Withdrawing into a protective cocoon and striking out by finger-pointing or condemning others are all examples of counterproductive behaviors.

Remember that when you express your opinion and the reasons behind it, you are not attempting to change beliefs; you are merely increasing the understanding of others so that they can internalize and make a choice to change or alter their own opinions, behaviors, and, yes, perhaps even their beliefs on a certain topic.

Hiding your differences creates an energy drain and leads to trust issues. Trust issues affect agreement, which affects costs. Lack of agreement among coworkers negatively impacts the bottom line.

Most people want to be part of a great company. I know that has always been a key "care-about" for me. I bet if you think about it, just for a moment, it's a "care-about" for you as well. I also think that you can play a part in making your company great.

Having been part of a great company like Texas Instruments (TI) for many years, I have had the opportunity to work with and around some great people. The common thread of these people is an overwhelming sense of self. They believe in themselves and what they can do. They share a part of who they are with the company so that the company can continue on a path of success.

If you are experiencing self-doubt, for whatever the reason, you are limiting yourself, which, in turn, limits the company. You are not fully engaged, and so you cannot help move the company to a higher level.

I recall a group meeting at TI that took place in 1998. An external diversity consultant was the facilitator, and the topic of gays came up. The context of the meeting was areas of diversity that cause the most discomfort. During one point in the discussion, one of my colleagues said to the group that she did not mind working with a gay person, but she would not have him or her over for dinner. The room got very quiet.

At that moment, I decided that I would come out to the group.

I said, "I am gay."

My colleague was shocked, as was the majority of the work group. There was a brief uncomfortable silence, and then the meeting continued.

After the meeting the colleague who had made the comment came up to me and apologized. She indicated that she just did not know anyone who was gay—other than me, of course, but she had not known it—and she felt uncomfortable. The two of us talked about the situation, and we began to build a more authentic relationship as time went by. Through the years, we have developed a very trusting and respectful relationship. She has since participated in professional LGBT events.

We all have the power to change things for the good or for the bad. The outcome of her comments could have been very different if I had remained silent or if I had demanded that she be disciplined for the comment. Neither of those responses would have helped the company, her, or me.

Lack of full engagement costs corporate America billions of dollars annually, and I believe it costs individuals in lost salary growth. Even a 1 percent improvement should be worth the effort. It should be worth the effort for the individual and the company to put some energy into enhancing a work environment that enables full inclusion—an environment that encourages people to be who they are.

Whether it's being denied the right to serve your country or the right to equal pay for equal work, injustice is all around us. It's hard to effect any change to the situation if you are not your whole self. If you are not fully present. What's important here is to break the cycle of silence.

The Situation

Carol, a twenty-five-year-old white female whose family was from one of the lower socioeconomic levels (i.e., financially stressed), has been with APD Corporation for only a short time. She graduated near the top of her high school class and was the only one of her five siblings to attend college.

She loves her work at APD and feels she fits in. Her work group is made up of what some would call WASPs and yuppies. They come from upper-class backgrounds and highly educated families.

Carol just never talks about her family. She finds herself becoming quiet when coworkers talk about their families, and she even excuses herself from conversations when it looks like there might be some probing into childhood experiences.

Early one Monday morning in a marketing campaign brainstorming meeting, Carol's work team was struggling with how to market an upscale product to a broader consumer base.

The team, based on their limited exposure to an economically diverse culture, kept coming up with marketing plans that Carol knew were too narrow. She remained silent through most of the meeting. When she did offer an idea, it was similar to others. She did want to offer the team the understandings derived from her background, but she was reluctant to reveal that she came from a lower socioeconomic level. She was deeply conflicted, and time was running out. The deadline for completing the campaign was fast approaching.

The Challenge

Carol has never discussed her background and is not comfortable about bringing her total self into the discussion. However, she has had different life experiences from her coworkers, and her exposure to an economically diverse set of people is something that she could leverage to help bring the team out of their narrow tunnel. What should she do?

Options and Probable Outcomes

Option 1: Carol continues her current behavior.

Carol remains silent, afraid to reveal her background—her true self—

because she worries that she will no longer be accepted within the company culture.

The probable outcome is that the team will continue to be limited, not only in this particular situation but in others as well. The richness of what Carol can bring to the table will remain hidden, and the team and the company will wind up losing—and Carol herself will lose too.

Option 2: Carol decides to speak out.

Realizing the limitations in the team's view, and the benefit that they and the company will receive because of her perspective, Carol speaks up, drawing upon her own experiences.

The probable outcome is that the team will be able to hear firsthand how an idea or image might be interpreted by another group that they don't personally have exposure to. Carol will be able to expand their knowledge and bring more value to the company and to each of the team members. Rather than lowering her status in the group, she'll find that her team members view her difference as a positive.

Self-Improvement Tips

For the Individual

On a routine basis, make a point to share something different about you and your experiences. Do this with a coworker you feel comfortable with. Branch out to others when you feel ready. Use each discussion as an opportunity to learn about others. Pretty soon you will find that you are building a comfort network.

Perhaps in the next meeting when ideas are being floated, float one yourself. Perhaps yours will be the one selected. Be sure to base your idea on your own truth and your own life experiences.

What Can a Manager Do?

Encourage your employees to share their stories with other coworkers. I realize that this may make some people uncomfortable. Some people may believe that this invades privacy. Of course, if you attempt to probe too deeply it can become a problem. What I'm suggesting is to provide a forum for people to share a little bit about who they are and where they are from. You can initiate the process by providing insights into your own background and life.

Once coworkers have a basic knowledge of each other's backgrounds, they can begin to find the connections and start to build relationships. When this happens, people will feel more comfortable drawing upon their life experiences and bringing those reference points into problem-solving situations. All this further fuels diversity of thought.

The Manager as Mentor

Reach out to a member of your staff who seems reticent to offer opinions or enter into the give-and-take of team discussions. Find time for the two of you to meet informally, perhaps over coffee, and encourage him or her to share more and to offer more insights and perspectives for the benefit of the team.

Summary of Situation

The strength of an organization lies in the strength of its people. It's the collective life experiences of the team that produces more comprehensive plans and associated action. Never minimize what your life experiences can add to organizational outcomes.

Idea #3

Assume Good Intentions— Breaking the Cycle of Mistrust

*Believe in yourself and in everything you can be…
not only will you be happy, but you will be able to
appreciate the good qualities of the people around you.*

—James Garner
Actor

Just as you must be aware of that internal voice in your head that is constantly undermining your confidence, you also must be aware of the internal voice regarding others. What do you find yourself saying to yourself about other people? When you see a woman who is aggressive, do you tell yourself that she must just be a bitch or that she is probably a lesbian? When you see a pregnant woman in the workplace, do you think she should not be there? That she should be at home? When you see a white man, do you think you can't trust him?

Whatever you are telling yourself, the first thing to do is recognize what the voice is saying. Next, get in touch with what is driving your thoughts. The voice you are listening to is usually rooted in your own experiences or the experiences of others close to you. There was a snub, a put-down—real or perceived—and perhaps even a physical encounter with somebody. Maybe it was just a warning against "those types of people."

Perhaps the event occurred so far back in your past that the memory is gone; it lives only as a negative reaction toward anyone who looks like them, acts like them, talks like them.

When you hear that internal voice telling you to mistrust someone's motives or abilities, attempt to assume the best of the individual. I don't want to make this sound easy; it's not. The mind's impressions, which the internal voice constantly echoes, are deeply etched, and it is not easy to let go of them.

However, it is not until you understand what triggers your thoughts that you can actually address them. Usually, the basic issue at the core is trust. Either you trust certain people or you do not, based on the filters through which you view them. It's easier to trust a person who is more like you. That is, unless you believe that you are not trustworthy. If you make up your mind not to trust people before really getting to know them, how can you expect them to trust you? And then, if you don't allow others to trust you, you are not giving yourself the chance to prove your own trustworthiness. It's a vicious cycle.

Think about what filters you view others through, as well as the filters you want others to view you through. Do you look at Christians as having a hidden agenda? Do you look at gays and lesbians as immoral, Hispanics as lazy, Muslims as terrorists? The list goes on.

Attempt to not think in terms of why you don't trust a person. Instead, think in terms of what you need to do to trust this person. How can you reach out with a trusting nature and thereby ensure that your own trustworthiness is demonstrated? I submit that when you reach out in a trusting nature, your own trustworthiness level goes up.

Now, if you find that your trust is misplaced because the person betrays you, that's a key learning moment. You can then alter your behavior with that specific person, based on facts. Nevertheless, attempt to keep in mind that the characteristic of that individual is not characteristic of the group that he or she belongs to.

Should you believe your trust has been betrayed, a solid approach is to discuss the situation with the person whom you thought you could trust. This conversation needs to be about the issue at hand, not about the person. It could be that extenuating circumstances caused the situation. You won't know unless you are willing to peel back the layers of the situation in order to get the facts.

Oftentimes, people will not make the effort to get the facts. The tendency is to feed the internal voice with a confirmation that, indeed, you cannot trust a person like that, and then you feel justified to continue with your labeling. This, too, is a cycle: the cycle of mistrust.

The Situation

For many years, Robert and Luke both have worked at Vintage Inc. Robert is a member of the Christian Values Employee Resource Group. Luke is a member of the Lesbian & Gay Employee Resource Group. These are but two of many employee resource groups at Vintage.

Robert and Luke know of each other and are aware of each other's involvement in their respective groups. They know that they are both thought of highly by company management.

However, Robert and Luke have not had an opportunity to work with each other until now. Based on their stellar track record of performance in project management, they have been selected to co-lead a major project. This project is very important to the company and could mean a great deal for the two of them if it is successful.

Robert and Luke meet to discuss how to proceed with the project. In the meeting, Luke quickly rejects Robert's plans for the project, dismissing them without an explanation. Robert is becoming very frustrated with Luke's rejection of his ideas. His initial feeling that the pairing of the two of them to colead this project was a mistake is growing stronger. He is considering going to his manager for reassignment.

Luke is dismissive of Robert's ideas, as he really mistrusts Christians. He sees them as attempting to control what people should think, how they should feel, and the way they should act. Robert just wants to get through the project as quickly as possible because he does have some discomfort working with a gay person.

Robert does not dislike Luke. He actually thinks he is very bright and hardworking. He just does not want to get too close to him, as he might be drawn into personal conversation, which is usually what happens with other people he works with closely. He feels that the longer the project goes on, the more likely it is for that to happen. He feels that just listening to Luke comment about what he and his life partner did over a weekend would convey consent of a lifestyle that his faith does not condone.

The Challenge

In this situation, it appears that Luke does not trust Robert, as he is not willing to acknowledge his ideas as having any merit. Robert may also have some trust issues, as he wants to either get through the project quickly or jump ship quickly. How can their discomfort with one another be overcome so that they can work together effectively for the benefit of the company and their own advancement?

Options and Probable Outcomes

Option 1: Robert could request a reassignment.

This would allow Robert—and Luke—to escape the problem rather than find a way to resolve it. Reassignment would only postpone the inevitable.

The probable outcome is that this will happen again for Robert, as well as Luke, on other projects in which they may not have a high level of comfort and trust for the other person.

Option 2: Robert could request to open a dialogue with Luke.

Robert could ask Luke to hear him out regarding the project ideas and then ask Luke to provide his ideas, at which point Robert will extend the same courtesy to Luke. Once all the ideas are out on the table, they would have a basis to compare and contrast their different approaches and find common areas of agreement. They both could also agree to an appropriate procedure for a vetting of their ideas by knowledgeable colleagues, provided that this is workable within the committed timeline for completion of the project.

The probable outcome is that they will find some common areas to agree on, and that commonality might provide a foundation for trust and comfort with one another, which, if it grows over time, would allow the project to move forward.

Self-Improvement Tips

For the Individual

Journaling is a good technique for self-improvement. When you hear yourself making judgments about yourself, write them down. When you hear yourself making judgments about others, write those down as well.

Revisit your journal on a routine basis in order to see if you discover a pattern of thought/behavior that looks first for the points of opposition. If you see such a pattern, attempt to change the behavior so that you look first at the commonality. In other words, focus on similarities, not differences. This is the way to build trust.

What Can a Manager Do?

A manager could reassign one or both of them and then name two new co-leads. This would most likely fuel the mistrust between Robert and Luke, and it might even cause bigger issues if Robert and Luke went on to share their mistrust with others. There would also be no assurance that a similar situation would not recur.

The better approach is to bring Luke and Robert together to share their ideas with you. Reinforce the ideas that you believe to be solid and then guide them to find the commonalities in their thinking that will allow the project to move forward.

The Manager as Mentor

During appropriate meetings, provide examples of people of different backgrounds and beliefs who found the means to overcome their difference to get to common ground. If possible, highlight examples from your own life experiences where individuals and/or teams have worked through trust issues and disagreements to achieve success. Highlight the approaches used that you believed proved to be the most helpful, emphasizing that people often have differences that can cause trust issues, but those differences can be overcome and must not be accepted as an excuse for failure.

This begins to reinforce an expectation of success, and above all, the awareness that people of differing backgrounds and beliefs can work together successfully.

Situation Summary

In any organization, you will find varying backgrounds rooted in strong beliefs. Attempting to change people's lifestyles is a road to disaster. Focusing on common beliefs and common goals will move you and the organization to a higher level of performance.

Idea #4

Develop Empathy for Others— Breaking the Cycle of Judgment

Put yourself in the other man's place; and then you will know why he thinks certain things and does certain deeds.

—Elbert Hubbard
Writer, Publisher, Artist, and Philosopher

It may be difficult for someone in a majority position to understand and appreciate the requests—sometimes demands—for change made by those in the minority.

"What's their problem?!"

"They're always bellyaching about something!"

"I'm tired of listening to their complaints!"

"They think they're entitled to more than the rest of us!"

"They'll never be satisfied!"

You've surely heard comments like these. Maybe you've even made them yourself about requests from minority groups other than your own. Think about your response to political or companywide activism on behalf of Hispanics or blacks or Muslims or LGBT or women, to use a few examples of minorities.

It's easy to become self-righteous and indignant over what you perceive to be outrageous demands by others. It's not so easy to place yourself in someone else's position in order to understand their issues. There's a lot of truth in that old saying about needing to walk a mile in another's shoes to fully understand where they're coming from and why they feel the way they do.

It's not easy to get out of your head and into someone else's, especially if those "someone elses" seem to be different from you and aren't people you're normally in contact with. But, as someone who is also in a minority position, you should have greater sensitivity—even empathy— for other minorities facing judgment, disapproval, and discrimination.

So, when afforded the opportunity, will you stand up for them? If you sympathize—perhaps even empathize—with them and their struggles, will you speak up, pointing out to colleagues and coworkers the obstacles faced by "those people" and why, based on your own experience as a minority, you believe their requests might have legitimacy?

What if you don't believe their requests are legitimate? Will you at least reach out to dialogue with members of that other minority group so as to better understand their perspective concerning their issues and needs? While that may not change your mind completely, it may provide you with some insights you hadn't considered that you can share with friends and coworkers.

If you won't speak up for other minority groups—or at least try to meet with them to better understand their needs—do you have a right to expect others to speak up for you and your group when you are the ones asking for fair treatment and change?

The Situation

Gary has been a single dad for a number of years and has held a fairly demanding job for as many years. Gary has managed to stay involved in his children's active lives. He ensures he gets them where they need to go: one practice to another. Gary also attends parent/teacher conferences and feels it important that the family sits down together for meals.

Through the years, he has built up a network of friends and neighbors who help from time to time when the schedule gets a little too crazy. Gary has kept his situation to himself at work. He's not attempting to hide anything; he just does not see a point in everyone knowing he is a single dad. Some of his golf buddies are aware that he is a single dad, but it's never really discussed. The closest they come to discussing it is joking around that Gary needs to spend more time practicing and perfecting his golf game.

Gary has heard many critical comments from male colleagues regarding how women expect to be treated differently in the workplace because they are moms. He has heard them scoff at the Working Mothers award that the company has received. Some of the comments have even come from senior leaders of the company.

He mainly hears this when he is on the golf course with them early on Saturday mornings—that is, when Gary can get away. He empathizes with working mothers and thinks to himself, *If my colleagues only knew what it takes for me to be here, then they would understand.* Then, he thinks, *No, they'll just think I'm whining, make a joke of it, and stop inviting me to play.*

The Challenge

The situation Gary finds himself in is that he could add a very different perspective to the table—that of being male, a dad, and the caregiver at home—if he would open up and allow others to see what a struggle it can be. However, he fears the potential negative consequences.

If Gary speaks up, he worries that his male colleagues will think he is suggesting that he wants special treatment or that he wants them to feel sorry for him.

Gary is not sure what he should do.

Options and Probable Outcomes

Option 1: Gary remains silent.

Thinking he has no choice, Gary decides to say nothing.

The probable outcome is that Gary will continue to struggle in silence, enduring the remarks that he hears from others—and growing increasingly resentful. The company may continue to have employees that are uninformed of the struggles of primary caregivers, be they women or men. In this situation, no one wins.

Option 2: Gary attempts to "come to the rescue" by telling his colleagues to chill with their comments.

He suggests to them that they need to align with the company's view on working mothers and be glad that they work for a company that recognizes the challenge of working mothers: a company that values the contribution of these women. After all, wouldn't they want their wives to be treated the same way?

The probable outcome is that his colleagues will stop listening and tune him out. No one likes to be lectured to. If people don't understand your perspective, you don't have a platform. They don't get the connection, so you sound like a "company man." What they hear is, "Just do it for the company; act a certain way while you are inside its walls." No progress is made; in fact, you might lose ground and damage relationships.

Option 3: Gary recognizes the comments of the others and suggests that they think about the situation in different terms.

He asks, "What if you were the primary caregivers?"

He opens a dialogue, asking the men if they would feel that they were getting special treatment, or if they would think that they just wanted flexibility and understanding from the company. He then lets them know of his situation and how helpful it has been to have a company that values his contribution and gives him flexibility to have a career and be a dad. He acknowledges that his situation is different in that he is the only parent. He goes on to tell them that the struggles of being the primary caregiver are real and that it is not just an issue for women.

The probable outcome is that he may move their thinking in some form or fashion. It's hard to tell. But what he did do was help himself and his company by putting a different perspective on the table. He also may find that others, both men and women, will come to him to share their struggles with balancing work and life responsibilities. In the end, they will all grow as individuals, which should add more value to the company.

Of course, he may find that he has unwittingly freed up his Saturdays.

Self-Improvement Tips

For the Individual

In most, if not all, situations, ensuring that people understand your perspective and the reasons behind it is the first solid building block to creating trusting relationships. Give people the benefit of the doubt and let them in on your thoughts.

What Can a Manager Do?

Attempt to stay in tune with what your employees might be struggling with from a standpoint of balancing work and life. You don't need to know everything about their lives, just enough to understand what they might be juggling. You may not be able to help address the situations as they arise; however, the knowledge gives you more insight into your workforce and it will send a message that you do care.

The Manager as Mentor

Be open to discussing your own situation. Offer insights into your life experiences, not just your work experiences. Let people in on your positive coping strategies for balancing work and home.

This helps you to be more genuine in the eyes of your employees, and it may open communication among them, thus allowing them to build stronger relationships with each other, which in turn will build stronger teamwork for the company.

Last, but not least, be willing to listen twice as much as you say.

Situation Summary

Strategies are part of human nature: what women should do and be, what a real man does or does not do, etc. As individuals, we should seek to understand stereotypes, to embrace the concept that they do not always hold true, and to acknowledge that our ability to see through them allows us to open our minds to the possibility of effecting meaningful change.

Idea #5

Deliver Results—Breaking the Cycle of Entitlement

Five percent of people make things happen; ten percent of people get involved with what is happening; and eight-five percent of people walk around saying— what's happening. Be part of that five percent.

—Dr. Jocelyn Elders
Fifteenth Surgeon General of the United States (1993–94)

Now, I know what you are thinking: *I don't feel entitled. Who does he think I am?*

I don't mean to offend anyone, but the truth is, some individuals *do* feel entitled. They feel that just because they are who they are, the company they work for has to offer them this or that. The truth also is that in some instances, by law, a company must do exactly what these individuals expect. A company must offer fair work practices and must not discriminate in their employment practices.

However, companies do not have to offer employee initiative or affinity groups. They don't have to honor Black Heritage Month; Hispanic History Month; National Coming Out Day, Ramadan, or the Chinese New Year. Companies do these things because management believes that such practices contribute to a better work environment. That they in turn lead to a more competitive position for the company. But do they really?

I submit to you that these practices do indeed contribute to a more positive environment where people want to do their best work, which translates to more value. However, this only happens when participants of the groups highlighted make a difference, and only if those participants help deliver results greater than those that they would have delivered otherwise. In other words, those participants must deliver results and deliver them in a way that boosts the bottom line.

That sounds pretty demanding doesn't it? It sounds like we have to deliver more than our nonminority counterparts. Well, in my mind, we do. We do have to step out, bring attention to what makes us different, and then illustrate how our difference can improve the bottom line.

So, if you are Hispanic, and your company markets to the Hispanic community, help the effort. Even if your job is not in marketing, do whatever is needed to optimize marketing efforts. The same is true for blacks, women, Asians, Arabs, etc.: find the connection and do something positive with it.

If your job is working on the loading dock, figure out how to get that truck unloaded faster by putting that creative mind to work—regardless of how outrageous your idea may sound. The worst idea is the idea never spoken, as there is no chance that idea will ever be implemented. High achievement requires an emotional investment.

I don't believe it is true that being part of a minority means you have to work harder, smarter and faster or that you need to work longer hours. It does mean that you give the time to make your difference, make a difference.

Today in the workplace, I do not waste energy attempting to hide. However, I do choose when to openly express my gayness. It's a matter of determining when it would help or hurt the work at hand. You must never let your difference be an excuse for not getting great results. Don't miss your opportunity to make a difference.

The Situation

Mario has just joined the company and is feeling excited about all the possibilities. He has gotten off to a great start and is already getting noticed by management. He is an entry level computer programmer but feels that he can make a bigger impact if he joins some of the employee initiatives. Because of his Mexican heritage, he feels that getting involved with a Hispanic employee group will allow him to build a personal network that can help him navigate the company more easily, enabling him to accomplish more, which will benefit both him and the company. He also just wants to meet people with similar backgrounds and interests. He goes to his boss and asks how he might connect with the Hispanic Employee Resource Group (ERG).

His boss responds by indicating that Mario might want to reconsider getting involved in anything that might distract him from his core work. "After all, Mario, you have only been at the company a few short weeks," his boss remarks, suggesting that Mario wait awhile before getting involved in any extracurricular activities at the company.

Mario is torn because he wants to join the initiative and meet people who share his background but is afraid to go against his boss. What if he joins the Hispanic ERG and then his work fails to meet his boss's expectations? In all likelihood, his boss will likely attribute it to his involvement with an ERG and then blame him for not following his advice. Mario is just not sure what to do.

The Challenge

As an individual, your challenge is how to know when it is appropriate to become involved in activities beyond your core job. As a manager, your challenge is how to best support employees' desires to become better connected without having it lessen their ability to perform the core job.

Options and Probable Outcomes

Option 1: Mario reluctantly follows his manager's suggestions.

Although he really wants to explore the Hispanic ERG, he doesn't; nor does he get involved in any extracurricular activities. He stays totally focused on his job.

The probable outcome is that Mario will become dissatisfied with his job, his boss, and the company. Mario will continue to do a good job. He will get things done but will not give of his discretionary time. He will only do what is necessary, never "going the extra mile" for the job or the company. Mario may even end up leaving the company as he begins to build more connections outside the company than inside it.

Option 2: Mario is honest with his manager, sharing his feelings in a respectful, company-oriented way.

He tells his manager that he wants to give the ERG a try, but should his work start to suffer, he will remove himself from the diversity initiative. His manager agrees, recognizing Mario's intention to make his job performance his top priority. Mario joins the ERG and then immediately looks for ways that his involvement can benefit the company.

The probable outcome is that Mario will go on to do a great job, willingly giving his own discretionary time to the job, as well as other activities that benefit the company. He will begin to bond with employees in the initiative, and that will enrich his personal life and greatly increase his job satisfaction.

Self-Improvement Tips

For the Individual

Seek clarity on expectations of performance. Don't assume anything. Leverage your company's performance management and individual development process as a personal improvement tool. Focus on your job first. Be careful not to over commit.

Seek feedback proactively. Key rule of thumb: don't let a quarter go by without a sit-down discussion with your boss. Take the feedback to heart. If you begin to slip on work output, cut back on your other activities.

Take full responsibility for your career, which means all the professional activities (inside and outside the company) that you are involved in. Always strive for a solid balance that gets the necessary results. Perform at expected levels at all times.

What Can a Manager Do?

Unless employees have existing performance issues, tell them to get involved to whatever extent they each desire. If issues come up along the way from a performance standpoint, don't assume they are because of the additional activities any employee is involved in. Address the specific performance concerns head-on, put a plan for improvement in place, and monitor progress.

The Manager as Sponsor

Be open to supporting new employees' involvement in extracurricular activities. This helps them establish supportive relationships at the company outside the immediate work team. This is good for retention. In the long run, you will have a happier, more productive employee.

If you see a dip in performance, address the specific issue related to the job in a timely manner. Don't make assumptions that it is related to these employees' involvement in initiatives inside or outside the company.

If you see solid performance on the job, as well as benefits accruing to the company through your employees' involvement in any initiatives, you should commend your employees and consider telling others in leadership positions about them, thereby opening the door for your employees' deserved advancement in the company.

Situation Summary

As employees, we all can benefit by getting involved in important activities outside our core jobs. In doing so, we grow by giving our discretionary time to broaden our experiences and connections with others. This allows us all to bring those experiences and connections back to the organization to help it grow.

Idea #6

———•◆•———

Cultivate Personal Credibility as a Bridge Builder—Breaking the Cycle of Blame

Personal relationships are the fertile soil from which all advancement, all success, all achievement in real life grows.

—Ben Stein
Writer, Actor, and Television Personality

The most important aspect of personal credibility in your job is your competence level. Competence in your job is king; know your stuff. In all likelihood, you were hired because of your education, your know-how, your past successes, or a combination thereof. All this is necessary, and it's what gets you to the table.

Now that you are at the table, what do you do? Unquestionably, you need to achieve results in your current work. Your competence means nothing if it does not translate into value and contribute to the bottom line. Having you on the payroll must be an advantage for the company.

Competence that translates into results is a ticket to the company dance. So now you are on the dance floor, dancing your heart out and showing all your technical ability and personal technique.

As you are dancing, you become very aware that there are others on the dance floor who are equally talented and accomplished. Some may be even more talented and accomplished than you are. So what characteristic can set you apart?

Consider the characteristic of being a bridge builder. Building personal credibility in the area of bridge building can be a true differentiator. How then can you build a reputation as a bridge builder?

First, tap into your background as a minority individual. In my own experience coming of age, I saw a lot of separation between various groups: blacks and whites, rich and poor, straight and gay. It was all around me. In my attempt to fit in, I tended to focus on what I had in common with various groups versus what was different between us. This just became a natural by-product of my personal makeup. Perhaps the same is true of you.

Bridge builders look for ways to connect. They focus on the commonalities without ignoring the differences.

An example of this happened at Texas Instruments (TI) when I was leading the LGBT Employee Resource Group (ERG). At the time, TI did not have a Christian Values ERG.

When a group of employees approached TI's Diversity Director to request that the company establish such an employee group, he wanted to ensure that the two ERGs would not pit themselves against each other.

He brought members of the LGBT group, myself included, together with representatives from the proposed Christian Values group.

The conversation focused on what both groups needed to achieve in order to move the company forward. We knew going in to the discussion that there were going to be differences in opinions and beliefs. The intent was not to attempt to change those opinions and beliefs, but, rather, to have a dialogue and establish a healthy understanding between the two groups.

Interestingly enough, as we focused on common goals for the company, we discovered that we had a lot of common beliefs. We found ways that we could support each other. An example of a common area was that neither group felt that religious beliefs or sexual orientation should be a reason for discrimination.

We all felt that employees should be assessed on their skills, abilities, and achieved results.

When we emerged from the dialogue, we felt that, indeed, we had a good example of bridge building. We shared this with the rest of the company by conducting a panel discussion with the leaders of both ERGs and key senior executives.

Since that time, the leader of the Christian Values ERG and I have participated in a couple of AIDS fundraising efforts together, walking alongside each other during an AIDS Lifewalk in Dallas.

I use this example to demonstrate how you can build your reputation and credibility as someone who can come to the table and move the company forward despite clear challenges. In fact, overcoming those challenges enhances your reputation and credibility.

This one example has also fueled my own reputation through the years, opening doors for me to impact various initiatives within the company.

If you think about the flip side of this, the outcome could have been very different. We could have come to the table and focused on the differences. We could have challenged each other's beliefs. We could have spent hours debating who was right and trying to prove each other wrong. This is the cycle of blame.

We all know that the cycle of blame plays out each and every day among teams or between individuals. Had this been the outcome, we would not have moved the company forward. We would have been seen, rightfully so, as people who were ineffective in dealing with a challenging situation. This is not a reputation that you want to have. Do you want ineffective people on your sales team? Do you want division in your company? I think not.

This example illustrates how to move something forward as it relates to helping create a more inclusive environment in a company.

There are other examples that relate to leveraging your ability as a bridge builder in helping to move forward on a change in organizational structure, a change in work flows, a change in business processes, and so on.

Typically, if you are effective at dealing with highly emotionally charged situations, it is indicative that you are effective in other high stakes situations as well. Others typically view bridge builders as people of high character and integrity.

LGBT people face issues every day that challenge their ability to build bridges, as they typically have to expose more of themselves in the process. Ethnic individuals may feel like they are giving away a piece of themselves in the process of attempting to see a white man's point of view. Or a man may feel like less of a man if he sees and supports the women's point of view.

I believe that if you are willing to take the higher ground as a bridge builder, the gains will far outweigh the potential downsides for you and your company. I think you will find that the more you give of yourself in the process, the more you and your company will get back.

You may even find that people will begin to seek you out as a bridge builder, and that they will want you on their team. Happy bridge building!

The Situation

Sally is a member of the women's ERG at her company. She is fairly active in the group, as she believes it helps to build women up in the company and provides good networking opportunities for learning and growth. She has seen the group help the company become a better place for women to not only do their best work but also to climb the corporate ladder. However, recently she has noticed the group becoming polarized in its views of work/life balance. She is very concerned about this.

Some in the group feel that the company should do more to ensure that women employees do not feel compelled to work long hours into the evening in order to compete with their male counterparts. Others feel that this is just part of the job and should be expected if the women are to compete with men.

Sally is torn and has not weighed in on the situation. She feels doing so would just add to the great divide that she sees coming.

The Challenge

It appears that Sally is not willing to step out and give her opinion as she typically does. She is not willing to do so, as she feels it may make matters worse and could damage her credibility with others in the group who may disagree.

Options and Probable Outcomes

Option 1: Sally remains quiet, hoping that the debate will go away.

Desiring to stay under the radar, she continues to quietly observe the combative discussions of her peers and coworkers, but she offers no opinions of her own.

The probable outcome is that the debate may go away with or without Sally's involvement. The risk for Sally is that the way she is handling this may become a pattern of behavior that could hurt her credibility and reputation in the long run. After all, people notice when a typically outspoken person suddenly becomes quiet and reserved. This may indicate to her peers that when the discussion gets tough, she bows out.

Option 2: Sally joins in the debate and firmly expresses her opinion.

Fighting her fear, she stands up and speaks out in her usual manner.

The probable outcome is that Sally's fear will become a self-fulfilling prophecy. She will likely alienate some who disagree with her, and the expression of yet another opinion, however honest it might be, will not move the group to a higher level of understanding, nor will it bring them any closer to closure.

Option 3: Sally acknowledges the different opinions but attempts to become a bridge builder.

She expresses her own opinion, but then she speaks to what she sees as common viewpoints from both sides of the argument. She acknowledges what the disagreements are and then helps to put them in perspective in light of what will help the company.

By focusing on the commonalities, her credibility goes up within the group. Groups tend to listen to the things they agree with.

Once she has them listening, she can then begin to tackle the lesser points of disagreement and work from there. Although this may require time and energy on Sally's part, it would prove to be very helpful to her in all aspects of her professional life.

The probable outcome is that the group will reach a level of agreement that keeps it working together and focused on the need to make progress in support of the company's work environment for women. The points of disagreement may still be there; they just won't become a barrier to progress. As people begin to work together on the commonalities, they will also begin to reach a better understanding of the differences.

Sally will then be seen as a problem solver because of her bridge building, and that is a highly valued attribute.

Self-Improvement Tips

For the Individual

First, have an opinion. Start by expressing it in terms of what you agree with, and then express the elements that you disagree with, explaining the reasons why. Once you have done this, if you feel it is appropriate and you are comfortable doing so, take the lead in helping a group or team members to do the same. Usually, when people understand the whys behind disagreements, they can better accept and respect those differing opinions.

Seek out an important issue for your company, as thorny as it might be, and tackle it head-on, looking for the common ground to build on.

What Can a Manager Do?

When you see situations like this playing out where people are going to their own corners and building on their opposing positions, be the person that brings out the commonalities. You might have to look hard for them, but they are there. If you can't get agreement in a timely manner and the delivery of a product or service is at risk, you will need to drive to a decision regardless of the disagreement. You can then come back and address some of the root causes on the disagreement at a later time.

The Manager as Mentor

If you see instances where a team is focused on the points of disagreement, whether it is a technical or a nontechnical issue, direct the group to the points of agreement and then work to eliminate the points of disagreement from that foundation. Over time, the team will begin to model that behavior on their own.

The Manager as Sponsor

As you observe your team members interacting to resolve conflicts and build bridges, you will likely find a team member who is particularly skillful in helping a diverse group of people reach common ground. Such an employee can prove valuable to the company, and you may want to sponsor that person as opportunities for advancement become available. Keep in mind that your sponsorship of a talented bridge builder will reflect positively on you.

Situation Summary

Building bridges across seemingly polarized views is hard work and is not for the faint of heart. However, people who do this will add tremendous value within their own organization, as well as outside of it. Honing the skill of bridge building as an individual contributor, a project leader, a supervisor, a manager, an executive, and even a CEO will increase your chances of succeeding in your endeavors.

Idea #7

Take on Issues Important to Your Company—Breaking the Cycle of "All About You"

Dedicate your life to a cause greater than yourself, and your life will become a glorious romance and adventure.

—Mack Douglas
Author

It is hard to not focus on yourself, your family, and your own little piece of the world. However, something other than you is at stake in the workplace: the company. This is not "You Inc."! You were hired by the company because you had the right stuff—or at least they thought you did.

We all know we spend a lot of time at the office, and it is easy to get caught up in the various political issues that typically go on within a company. You have one group of employees thinking that another group is treated better. One group feels another group is getting more attention, etc. … If any of that goes on in your company, rise above it.

If they are not going on, you should feel lucky. I assure you that the people who came before you must have paved the way, because progress does not *just* happen; people *make* it happen.

Remember that your job performance is your number-one priority. Once you have a clear focus and understanding in your job, begin to branch out. Focusing on issues and causes that are important to the company is the very key to your success. It is about understanding the broader context of the industry and communities in which your company operates. It's about understanding the various diversity aspects of your company. Just doing your job well is not enough.

Understanding this broader context should enable you to do a better job, or at least to be more committed to your work. When you expand your scope of interest in the company beyond your specific role—your position, your job—you start giving that extra discretionary effort to the company.

For me in my career at TI, I started to build an ownership for the company such that I wanted to enhance the brand of the company and become part of that brand. I started to build a positive image for myself within the company. The more you build on your positive personal image, the more it reflects a positive light on the minority group you identify with.

So how can you know about the important issues and causes? Ask. Your boss might be a good person to start with; or, perhaps, your HR manager. You might also find out by browsing your company's website. Once you educate yourself, look for ways that you can get involved and add value. In some cases, you might find that there is a direct relationship between the issue/cause and your job.

For example, perhaps you find that your company is involved in helping underprivileged children receive a good education. You role at the company is in the sale of computers and calculators. You offer your discretionary time to the company by going out to some of the schools and setting up tutoring sessions that leverage the company's products.

The mutual benefit is that the children now have access to tools that enable their education, and the company boosts its reputation and gains additional exposure of its products.

So what do you get out it?

By focusing on the areas important to your company, you bring a lot of focus on yourself, and you raise the collective positive image of your minority group. Keep in mind that being a minority and leveraging your talent inside and outside the company sends a positive signal to the company that it needs more people like you.

Also, keep in mind that you are representing your company, and that your comments must always reflect a supportive nature while at the same time reflecting your unique perspective.

If you find yourself in a role that allows opportunities for you to speak about your company at an external event, you might consider reflecting on what it is like to work as a minority at your company. This can apply to any minority—black, Hispanic, gay, woman, etc. You might consider making a point to comment on the diversity within your company and the supportive culture.

Even if you feel that more needs to be done—and there always is more to be done—your supportive comments can move initiatives forward. Your comments can boost your own image, as well as your company's image. You start bringing the brand of the company to life through the person you present yourself to be.

Aligning your interests with the company is key. It is worth repeating that the other way around usually does not work. Trying to align your company to your way of thinking is a battle you just might not want to fight.

Now, that's not to say that you should not speak up if you discover that something wrong or unethical is going on at your company. By all means, speak up in such circumstances.

However, if you feel your company can do more in the area of accommodating the Asian culture for certain holidays, find out who can affect the decisions regarding the corporate culture, arrange a meeting, and then build your case. The case should be presented from the perspective of what is good for the company. Usually, this type of appeal is most successful when prepared with the help of the appropriate employee resource group (ERG) or employee minority network (EMN), if your company has such a network.

If your company does not have these types of employee groups/ networks, you might consider starting one.

If you decide to get involved in such a group/network, or even to start one, always look for synergy, as this is essential to any endeavor— that is, synergy between you, the rest of your minority group, and the company. If you can't find synergy, it probably is not the right thing to be pushing, or it is not the right time. Whatever it is, know when to correct your course.

In the mid-1990s, I began to get involved in the Dallas AIDS Lifewalk and wanted to approach TI about becoming a corporate sponsor of the event. I knew it might be a challenge, as the company only sponsored a Juvenile Diabetes Walk and a Breast Cancer Walk. Other than those events, United Way was the only corporate-giving activity.

Knowing that AIDS was not a health issue understood or embraced by the majority, I approached senior management and made an appeal, illustrating the connection between this health issue and the need to sustain a healthy worldwide employee base, short- and long-term. I tied the issue to the bottom line of the company, highlighting the financial impact of lost productivity. That made the connection between an issue important to my minority group and its potential impact on the company.

The connection had synergy.

I then expanded that connection to the majority, pointing out that AIDS and HIV have affected millions of people just like them and their family members. I found that building that common connection was a bridge to their understanding.

That was more than fifteen years ago. Texas Instruments (TI) and its foundation have since contributed thousands of dollars to this health issue. In 2008, TI received an award for its efforts.

This started with painting the picture of the value to the company and led to the company's receiving the value. In addition, many people impacted by AIDS/HIV have benefited from TI's involvement.

Always keep in mind that diversity alone does not build advantage; it's what you do with the diversity that builds advantage. You must constantly look at your ideas as building value for the company. A company, like an individual, wants to invest in things that have a return.

Show the return, and you will more than likely get the backing. Sometimes you can't show a return. Sometimes it is just a leap of faith that a company chooses to take. However, a company is more likely to take that leap of faith if an employee minority group within the company displays strong advocacy and commitment to the cause at hand.

An example of a leap of faith might be when a company expands its nondiscrimination policy/equal employment opportunity (EEO) statement to include additional groups, knowing that this expansion is not supported in the mainstream and could invite criticism. For example, gender identity and/or gender expression.

However, company leaders may move forward because of the overriding message it sends: the message of full inclusion. A company usually does not make a change like that without seeing some level of passion from within the company.

A company might make such a change if they see the passion within you and/or your minority group. When companies add gender identity and gender expression to their EEO policies, you can bet that some voices from an employee minority group have already built the business case.

Note that I said *business* case. As the specific issue of gender identity and expression may only affect a very small portion of any workforce, a company may elect to expand the policy because one person or an employee group made the case that it is not about gender, it is about inclusion. Having an inclusive workplace is good for business.

Don't be shy about helping to drive change. Not only could it help change your company for the better, it could also make it a stronger company *because of you*.

The Situation

Scott is highly proficient in his job and has for many years been ranked at the top of the organizations he has been a part of. Currently a manager within his work group, he is often asked to take the lead on projects that span across his boss's organizations. He is a gay man and is out at work only to those he is closest to. He has been very reserved about letting the world know that he is gay.

Scott knows his company has a nondiscrimination policy that includes LGBT. He also knows that it is important to the company that all employees feel they can be who they are at work, with no need to hide what makes them different.

He understands that it is important to the image of company for the outside world to know what the company is doing to embrace inclusion and diversity.

However, he still feels that within the company, being gay is more of a liability than an asset. He senses that coworkers really don't want to know his orientation, as they never ask about his outside interests or even about his family or friends. He does not think he is working in fear because he knows he is valuable to the company, based on what he brings to the table.

He continues to get public acknowledgments and kudos from his superiors. Because of this, he does not give much thought to what other LGBT employees feel or what their experiences might be.

As a result of all this, Scott continues to avoid open support of the LGBT efforts within the company, believing that someday, if things change for him, he can be more out in the workplace, and then become actively involved in and supportive of company efforts in this arena. But for now, he needs to sit back.

The Challenge

Scott may truly be okay with people discovering he is gay, and he may honestly believe that his involvement in LGBT efforts would bring no additional value to the company. In that case, there is no real issue here. However, if it is a situation of fear and outward discrimination that is happening within his company, regardless of corporate diversity policies, that is altogether different. If the latter is the case, it is an issue that needs to be addressed, and Scott needs to do some serious soul-searching about his reluctance to become involved.

Options and Probable Outcomes

Option 1: Scott continues to do his job, and he does it well.

He does not open up about his sexual orientation. If it becomes known and then becomes an issue, he will address it—but not until that happens, if it happens.

The probable outcome of this is that he will go on as he has up to this point, and the company will do likewise. It will take other gay managers and/or leaders to make the company better. It will not be Scott. Scott and the company both will lose out on the opportunity.

Option 2: Scott continues to focus on his job, doing it well as he has for many years, but he also explores doing something positive for the LGBT community of which he is a part.

He does not change his approach to coming out at work, per se; instead, he looks for a way to incorporate an issue that is important to his minority group (in this case, LGBT) and attempts to make a positive change that will fuel the positive image of his company and what they are doing in that arena.

Perhaps Scott can highlight what his company is doing as part of its journey toward overall diversity/inclusion—whether he is with a customer or a supplier, at a speaking engagement, or at any outside venue. Or he can take on an issue that is heavily valued by the LGBT community and attempt to get the company to become a corporate stakeholder. For example, the AIDS/HIV health issue.

The probable outcome is that Scott will quickly become a positive voice for both the company and the LGBT community. By doing this, Scott will raise his value to the company, as he will contribute to its brand in a positive way. Eventually, he might even feel comfortable about coming out, as he and his company will have seen the benefit of his efforts.

Self-Improvement Tips

First, attempt to get in tune with how you really want your work life to be; what you really want the work life for others to be at your company. If you are truly okay with how things are, and you see no need for improvement, don't waste the time.

However, if you do see areas that need to improve, write down what you think your company could do better as it relates to the improvement of work life. Some of these things may or may not be related to feeling included or excluded based on a personal attribute.

Whatever they are, write them down; then narrow the list down to a core set of ideas and develop the value propositions from the company's perspective. Next, bounce the ideas off a select group of individuals whom you trust and whose opinions you value. If you see synergy and support, go to the company's decision makers and key influencers and present your idea(s). Be sure to show your passion for helping to drive the needed changes.

What Can a Manager Do?

As a leader or manager within your company, be in tune with your people. This does not mean that you are prying into their personal lives. It does mean that you care enough about them to know more about them than what they bring to the table at work.

Build followership. People want to follow leaders who really care about who they are, not just what they know.

The Manager as Sponsor

Make a list of your employees and ask yourself who you know really well. Jot down what you know about these individuals. See if you find consistency in the type of information.

Do you know their interests outside of work? Do you know anything about their family, friends, etc.? Think about the ones you know really well, and see if you find any correlation between their performance, their achieved results, and the opportunities that you send their way.

Compare that to the list of individuals you don't know so well. Study your findings, and if you see that the performance of those you know better is higher, work to fill in some missing information on those people you don't know very well.

Make it a point to reach out to them and get to know them better. After a while, compare the two groups to see if you start to see a narrowing margin of performance between them—or, at least, a narrowing margin of your perception of their performance. Stick with this method and see where it takes you. It just might cause you to engage in some self-reflection that helps improve your own performance.

Also, as you go through the process, ask yourself if there are reasons you have reached out naturally to some and not others. Be honest with yourself, as you might uncover some hidden bias that, if addressed, could make you not merely a good leader but a *great* leader.

Along the way, as you discover top talent, get involved in understanding what they need to develop, and then follow their progress. When you see opportunities in your group or another organization, highlight the individual for specific opportunities.

Situation Summary

In most everyone's job at a company, the ability to effect positive change usually exists, either in the way that work gets done or in the environment in which it gets done. All it takes to effect such change is having open eyes and an open mind. When you step out of your little corner of the company and see the bigger picture, you can start to see opportunities to make a difference for yourself and for others. The differences that you make may be very small, but they can lead to systemic change.

Idea #8

—◆—

Be a Voice for Your Company— Breaking the Cycle of Silence

It is through cooperation, rather than conflict,
that your greatest successes will be derived.

—Ralph Charwell
Author

This chapter may be easy for some and not others, depending upon where your company is in its diversity journey. If you feel that your company is making progress in the right areas, you may feel more compelled to be an ambassador. If you feel your company is not very progressive, you may feel otherwise. Either way, you can be a voice that will make a difference.

If your company is progressive in the area of work/life balance for working moms or single dads, let people know about it. If your company allows religious expression in the workplace, let people know about it. If your company offers domestic partner benefits, let people know about it.

Letting people know can take many different forms. It could be one-on–one, where you individually tell others what it is like to work for your company as a black, a woman, an Asian, a gay person, and so on.

You might also consider looking for opportunities to serve in a leadership capacity in an external diversity organization or chamber. This helps to draw your company in. Even though you might join as an individual, because you are part of a company, you are seen as a voice for your company. Even if you don't want to be that voice, you become it because of the association. Right or wrong, that is typically what happens.

What you say or do will reflect on your company. Make the best of it: present the most positive picture of you and the company.

If you like to speak to groups, you might look for opportunities to highlight what is going on within your company. Even if you believe there is still more to do, as there always will be, highlight the good things and acknowledge that progress has been made.

Whether you are talking one-on-one or speaking to a thousand people, always present a balanced view. Talk about what else needs to be done and how your company is progressing. Listeners usually appreciate a balanced view. Presenting "too rosy" a view will invite skepticism.

Internally, use every opportunity to align your diverse group to the needs of the company. Highlight areas where you feel diverse employees are making a difference.

If you can't seem to bring yourself to the point where you can give credit to your company for making progress, it might be time to find another company—for its sake and yours. Staying with a company that you feel is not making enough progress, or that you feel does not want to make progress, could spell disappointment for you long-term.

An important point to remember is that your goal is to bring your company along, not to take it on.

The Situation

Ellen has been with StarCup Industries for over ten years, and she enjoys her work very much. She feels very secure in her job and gets plenty of positive reinforcement about her work and her value to the company. She is Muslim, and although she feels comfortable being in a minority, she feels like her company should do more to help Muslins feel more comfortable in general in the workplace.

For example, during the period of Ramadan, she finds it very awkward to go into the ladies room to conduct her prayer. Other Muslim employees feel the same. However, they do feel that the company does a lot to embrace different cultures, and they are hesitant to ask for more for fear that they would just stand out more.

Ellen has just been elected as a board member of the local Muslim Business Chamber. Part of the process for new board members is for each to address the chamber's membership at one of their dinner meetings. Ellen is very excited about this, as she feels her qualifications and her background will help the chamber. She is also very proud of StarCup.

The night of the dinner meeting is full of excitement as the new Board members each present themselves and introduce their companies to the Chamber. It is now Ellen's turn to take the stage. Her introduction to the chamber membership is outstanding. It's obvious that she has the respect of the entire group and that she understands the mission of the chamber.

She discusses StarCup's business model, its markets, and its products. She also spoke of the wonderful work environment at the company. At the end of her presentation, she asks for questions.

One person asks why StarCup does not allow for the observance of Ramadan. "It seems odd for a Muslim to talk about such a wonderful corporate cultural when it's one that does not recognize such an important holy event," the other chamber member finishes.

As the room falls silent, Ellen listens to the question and comments, wondering what to do.

The Challenge

Ellen finds herself face-to-face with being a spokesperson for her company. She knows that what she says now will really matter, and she wants to represent her company and herself well.

Options and Probable Outcomes

Option 1: Ellen repeats all the things that StarCup has done to embrace the diversity of its employees.

She reinforces and acknowledges that StarCup is lagging in the area her colleague described. She further indicates that StarCup needs to step up to the plate and make Muslims feel more included, emphasizing that she plans to approach management in order to rectify this issue.

The probable outcome is that people will walk away with somewhat of a mixed or negative view of not only StarCup but Ellen as well. Her response will be perceived as weak and not reflective of her strong introductory comments.

Option 2: Ellen acknowledges the statement and indicates that the company will be addressing it in the near future; she thanks the audience and walks off the stage.

This response does not reflect Ellen or StarCup in a strong or positive light.

The probable outcome is that the person who asked the question will not be satisfied with the answer, and the entire audience will wonder why Ellen did not go into any detail. They may wonder if she is hiding something, and they may even wonder if she was authentic when making her opening remarks about StarCup.

Option 3: Ellen immediately acknowledges that StarCup has not addressed this issue, and in fact, it is something that the StarCup Muslim employees need to embrace and approach management to dialogue.

She then acknowledges that management is very open to the ideas of its diverse employees, citing examples of such openness. She mentions that she anticipates that making appropriate accommodations for employees to observe Ramadan will not be an issue.

The probable outcome is that the audience will acknowledge that the company would handle this request in the same good manner that they have handled others. Also, it is clear that Ellen has placed some ownership on the Muslim employees of the company, which is very important.

In fact, she may have given other Muslims the nudge they needed to approach their own companies. In this way, she is positively impacting the larger business community and simultaneously showing her own strong leadership skills.

Self-Improvement Tips

For the Individual

If you think you will find yourself in situations where you are speaking to a group as an informal representative of your company, ask your HR or PR department to recommend training on how to field questions.

If you are a member of an employee resource group, ensure that you are in tune with how the group works with management to bring about needed change. Get involved in the discussions and always align the "ask" with business impact. Express to decision makers the type of environment that brings out the best in your minority group. Don't be shy about this. They don't know what they don't know, so don't assume.

If you have a fear of public speaking, start with small groups and build from there. Find someone who is good at public speaking and ask for tips; see if that person will let you do a "dry run." Fear of public speaking can hold you back from making a larger impact for your company and your diversity group. It's not necessary, but it will be helpful in your overall career.

What Can a Manager Do?

Be aware of the cultural differences that abound in your organization. You don't have to be an expert in any one of the many aspects. Just being aware makes you more sensitive in your own calendar planning. For example, don't schedule meetings and other key events on days of minority observance, as doing so could send unintended messages of exclusion and/or discrimination. Also be supportive of changes that the company may need to make, and speak up about changes that you think should be made.

The Manager as Mentor

Be aware of what your employees are involved in outside of work that might draw the company in. Chambers are an obvious venue, but there may be others. Perhaps people are leaders in their homeowners associations, churches, temples, etc.

Being aware will help you coach them, as appropriate, to ensure they are better equipped to field questions when they come up. You can also help them make connections within the company that would benefit them in their external work, which in turn will benefit the company.

A side benefit of this is that the more you are aware of an employee's leadership outside the company, the greater potential you have to leverage that ability inside the company.

Situation Summary

Cultural perfection is impossible. There are too many nuances and customs to be 100 percent spot-on. The goal should be cultural awareness and sensitivity. As individuals and as companies, we should all strive to understand the cultural differences that exist in any organization, and to the extent possible, we should make accommodations suitable for the workplace. If you find that you just don't know much about the cultures represented around you, just ask. Most people are very happy to speak to you about their culture.

Idea #9

Be Flexible and Take Risks— Breaking the Cycle of Fitting In

*Unless you walk out into the unknown, the odds of making
a profound difference in your life are pretty low.*

—Tom Peters
Author

The business world changes often and quickly, based on economic conditions, industry and market conditions, as well as changing customer needs. You need to be aware of what is important to your company as it adapts to these changes. Even more important, you should be prepared to change with it. A business will need to change and adjust many factors in order to obtain the right focus. These factors include, but are not limited to business strategy, investment strategy, and human- and capital-resource strategy. What is important for you, the employee, is to know how your company is attempting to adapt and change in order to make the most progress with such essential constant factors as the focus on revenue, cost control, and profit. Remember, the bottom line is always the number-one priority.

Given all these changing forces and the uncertainty that they tend to bring with them, how can you bring your difference to the table to enable your company to achieve the best results? How do you position your difference as a positive for the company's bottom line, given these unavoidable prevailing forces? The answer is by staying flexible and taking some risks.

Flexibility can mean a lot of things. As someone who is different, I have become somewhat of a master of flexibility. When you are not in the majority, you typically adjust in order to align; you adjust your actions, your attitude, your appearance, and whatever else is necessary in order to achieve alignment. We learn that we must do this at an early age. Furthermore, I believe that alignment is a skill that most in the majority lack. Some might say that alignment means "fitting in," and fitting in is not necessarily a skill to be proud of. Even the name of this chapter suggests that one should not *just* fit in. However, I believe that the way in which you leverage the skill of alignment makes all the difference.

People tend to spend a lot of time singing the blues about the changing market conditions, the changing customer demands. People who possess the skill of alignment can reach into their past to remember how they were able to make the most of difficult times, how they learned to adapt to situations almost immediately. This skill gave them an edge.

Individuals who possess this skill don't spend a lot of time asking why things are happening. They spend the time asking what can be done, given the changing conditions, and then they start looking at how to align and adapt. As an individual contributor, a member of a team, or a manager, offer up suggestions early on that focus on the improvements and adjustments needed.

Then, if you are a member of a minority, perhaps go one step further. Go back to others like you and ask them to do the same. Rally the troops, if you will. If your company has employee resource groups (ERGs)—such as a Black ERG, a Hispanic ERG, and LGBT ERG,—appeal to the relevant group to come up with suggestions as to how the group can assist the company in its objectives. If you do this, keep in mind that any activity that the group suggests getting involved with is over and above what you are already doing in your job/role. Each member of the group will need to stay focused on their specific jobs as well.

Bringing to bear the power and capability of your ERG helps to shape the image of the group as a whole and deepens the impact that it can have. Focusing on the company objectives in times of great need helps to establish the value that the group has, as well as the value of each individual member of the group. This in turn will allow the group to help shape other aspects of the company that more directly benefit the ERG.

For example, if the Hispanic ERG is actively involved in helping the company address the changing consumer tastes in Latin America, when the ERG needs sponsorship during Hispanic cultural events, the company may be more willing to go the extra mile.

If the LGBT ERG helps the company address market issues in certain metropolitan areas across the country, when the ERG petitions the company for domestic partner benefits, they will have a better business case to support their request.

This is not the "good ole' boy/ you scratch my back, and I'll scratch yours" scenario. It is about good business sense. It's about leveraging all the power of a diverse workforce. It's about employees caring for the company, and the company caring about its valuable employees.

If you are continuing to use your alignment skill to just fit in, you probably will not see the changes or events around you. Don't do what

I did. I had to go outside my own company to find out that we had a fairly strong LGBT ERG at the company. I was so far back in the closet that I did not want to know. I did not want to fully leverage my skill. Instead, I used the skill and the associated energy to just fit in.

Oftentimes it is fear that causes us to just want to fit in. Sometimes this fear causes us to create blind spots that are not in our best interest or the best interest of our company. Helping your company see beyond its blind spots is great. But first, we each must see our own blind spots. Playing it safe and avoiding blind spots can take you down a path of mediocrity. It's important to acknowledge your fear and then move past it, creating clear sight for all the possibilities. In other words, instead of staying stuck in the way things are—the status quo maintained through fear and blind spots—imagine the way things could be. This requires courage, character, and integrity.

If you continue down a path of fitting in, you may find that you end up compromising yourself and your company. For example, let's say you are in the procurement organization of your company and you are also a member of a minority group. You are also very much aware of outstanding diverse suppliers, including those within your own minority group, but you don't speak up. You don't want to appear to be biased toward your minority group, so you do not call attention to a specific minority supplier. Or, you don't want anyone to know that you have any insight into a certain minority supplier network/chain. In doing this, you are actually compromising your company's ability to draw from that supplier base, as well as compromising your own identity with that minority supplier.

It is not about playing favorites by sticking up for a certain minority supplier because of your affinity with that minority, it is about bringing your full perspective to the table. By bringing your full perspective to the table and not attempting to assimilate, you can bring all relevant viewpoints to the discussion, thereby optimally leveraging the value of your difference. In this example, taking this approach helps to align the procurement organization's diversity supplier goals and objectives with your own personal passion, thus allowing you to be more effective. Bring all your difference to the table, and remember that being too cautious is the surest way to *not* make a difference.

The Situation

Terry, a design engineer at Cosmos Electronics, has been with the company for about ten years. In those ten years, he has seen the company grow in both revenue and market share. He is proud to be part of a company that has sound business strategy and that delivers valuable products to the market to make life better for so many. He loves working for the company, as he is allowed to innovate and create. He is aware that the company is currently facing some tough customer issues. It appears that the company continues to be fairly successful at growing revenue; however, in the past few years, it has not been able to grow market share as much as needed, especially in culturally diverse markets. What makes this situation worse is that even the revenue has recently begun to decline.

Terry hears management talk about these issues, including their recognizing the need to spend more time with customers. He is already aware that his own boss spends an enormous amount of time with the customer. Jack, Terry's manager, is always on the road visiting one customer after another. Terry's understands that his boss is not unique. He has heard that the sales force, as well as key business managers, also spend the majority of their time at customer locations in direct dialogue. He wonders what could be the issue.

Terry thinks to himself, *Hey, I'm just a designer; management will solve the issue.* However, he does wonder if management is truly adapting to the customers' needs, or if they are being inflexible. He has seen some inflexibility from the management team on some internal matters and wonders if that inflexibility is transcending to the customer as well.

The Challenge

The situation Terry faces is one of knowing when it is appropriate to get involved. It is so easy sometimes to say "not my job." For Terry, flexibility comes very naturally; he is a Hispanic gay man who has had to adapt to family and cultural pressures all his life. He has been successful at his job, and he is considered a key technical talent for his company.

Options and Probable Outcomes

Option 1: Terry keeps his head down and does his work in his usual excellent manner.

Terry continues to feel that management's inflexibility is at the root of the problem with the customer base, but he does not feel that it is his responsibility to address the issue.

The probable outcome is that the company will continue to struggle and potentially lose revenue and market share, thus causing the company to have to dramatically adjust resource levels. Terry may find himself out of a job, should things get bad enough to warrant staff cuts in product design. At a minimum, he may have to seek other employment if conditions worsen. Having to do this would disrupt his personal life. He loves the company, so this would be painful on multiple fronts.

Option 2: Terry goes to his boss and opens a dialogue on the issues.

He offers up some suggestions as to how the company might improve the way it builds customer relationships. He further offers to help by visiting a customer.

The probable outcome will depend on Terry's relationship with his boss, and that will account for differences in the reactions that his boss might have. For example, his boss might take exception to Terry's offer to assist. After all, the boss has been spending a lot of time with customers and so might assume that Terry is suggesting that those efforts with the customers are failing.

At best, Terry might be given the opportunity to interface directly with the customer and have a positive impact. That impact would be a step in the right direction, but not necessarily enough to have any type of a meaningful effect, as speed is important in the marketplace. Every day, revenue will continue to decline, and competitors will continue to take market share.

Option 3: Terry discusses the situation with his peers within the company.

He also brings the topic up for discussion with the various leaders of the company's ERGs to see if there is some sort of project that the ERGs can take on that would help with the situation. Terry is very much aware that each of the ERGs has had to bridge differences and tackle difficult inflexibility and trust issues. Terry helps assemble a subteam to make recommendations to management as to the things that they would be willing to do over and above their respective jobs in order to help address the customer issues.

The probable outcome of this will also likely vary. At worst, they may be told no. However, management would remember that the ERGs offered their assistance and that they were willing to come together on behalf of the company. It's hard to say no to such a show of company support.

The best-case scenario is that the sub-team of the ERGs will be able to help execute some sort of intervention that allows the company to gain more insight into customer issues related to diverse cultures, and this additional insight will, in turn, lead to more trust between the company and those customers. This optimal outcome will be a win-win situation for everyone.

Self-Improvement Tips

For the Individual

When you see issues that your company faces, offer up your assistance as an individual or as a member of an ERG or another type of sub-team. Be willing to recognize how you might bring a unique or different perspective to the table. Step out of your comfort zone and take a chance.

What Can a Manager Do?

When employees offer to assist over and above the great work that they are already doing, even when it might appear that they are seeing a gap in what may be your responsibility, embrace it! The worst thing you can do is be defensive. The best thing that can come of your welcoming the help is that you receive assistance with your own workload at the same time as you pump more energy into that employee. What a deal! You, your employee, and your company all benefit.

The Manager as Sponsor

If you have an individual or a team of people willing to tackle a tough business issue, on top of what they are already doing, stop and take notice. Barring any individual performance issues, let them do it. Stay involved with the individual or the team and give them some direction, but allow them the opportunity to view the problem through a different set of eyes. Always be open to the ideas and suggestions.

If you cannot let the team or individual assist, let them know why. By doing this, you build loyalty to the company, trust within your team, and trust between you and your team.

When someone on your team steps out and takes on important issues for you, and does so successfully, make sure that you highlight that individual in important discussions with the leaders in the company. This could make a huge difference for the individual and for you.

Situation Summary

Of all the attributes that one possesses, flexibility and adaptability are on top of the list for a successful career and business. If you cannot demonstrate these attributes, as an individual or as a company, you will not survive in the business world. The business world is far too dynamic to tolerate inflexibility or a lack of adaptability; rather, it demands rapid responses to the ever-changing market conditions. It's far less risky to make a change than to remain the same. If you remain where you are, you can bet that others within or outside your company will surpass you—or that the competition will surpass your company.

Idea #10

Focus on Progress—Breaking
the Cycle of Impatience

I've learned it's usually the little things that make a difference.

—John Gray, PhD
Counselor, Lecturer, and Author

The key is to focus on progress. Don't focus on nirvana: it doesn't exist. You need to focus every day on the next step you need to take in order to move ahead as an individual, as a group, as a company. There will always be something to work on—*always*.

Progress takes time. It's the journey, not the destination that counts. If you just stop and think of all the people and events that you influence during the journey, you can only start to imagine the impact that you may have had on others and their causes, on other companies and their journeys. Don't minimize your impact. Small things add up.

When I think about the journey, not the destination, I'm reminded of a conversation that my son Brandon and I had regarding his education. He had recently started attending the Engineering School at UT Dallas, after spending several years working at odd jobs and then attending community college.

Brandon's a very smart man with an internal drive to succeed. Shortly after starting the program in Dallas, he mentioned that he would like to obtain his degree at UT Austin, a more highly ranked school. I told him to keep his sights on it, and if he had the grades, perhaps it would be possible. Sounds good, right?

As time went on, we began to focus too much on the possibility of a transfer, to the point where his grades started to fall. We both had to reel ourselves in and take stock of all that needed to be accomplished in order for a transfer to even be a possibility.

This reevaluation did not happen until Brandon himself saw the need to refocus. Now he is focused on what he needs to do in the present that will better prepare him for future opportunities. This is a simple concept rarely heeded.

I can remember many years ago when the equal employment opportunity (EEO) policy at Texas Instruments (TI) was modified to include nondiscrimination coverage for gay and lesbian employees. How exciting that was. A few years later, the company added domestic partner benefits. The time between those events could have been longer, or it could have been shorter. Yes, there were two events. It's true that they could have occurred closer together or at the same time. But it's also true that neither event could have occurred. There could have been no modification to include gays and lesbians in the EEO policy in any way whatsoever.

It was through the efforts of a few that these events happened—the tireless efforts of not only a few gay and lesbian employees at TI, but also some supportive managers and leaders. Each of these individuals took on the challenge in a positive way, looking to change the company for the better, not to force social issues on the company. All this took time.

Several years later, the company once again expanded the EEO nondiscrimination policy to include gender identity and gender expression. In fact, it happened during the writing of this book. I do feel that my involvement in the effort to effect positive change made a difference.

During that process, it was key to focus on the positive change and movement ahead. It would not have added value to focus on the length of time it took to effect the change. You must stay the course and stay positive with any type of cultural change, as these changes do take time.

The key in proposing any change for your company is to focus on the benefit to the company and its employees. Don't focus on some external measure or index of where a company should be. Although indexes like the HRC Equality Index or the List of Best Places to Work for Blacks are highly important, they are not reasons to make a change. Higher scores do not make a great company.

Always keep the desired outcome in sight; don't lose sight of it, or you'll lose your focus. Just keep everything in perspective. If at any point during the journey you find that your desired outcome or destination is vastly different from your company's, correct your course by recalibrating so that you can achieve alignment with all the key stakeholders. If you feel you can't, realign your personal goals and objectives regarding the matter at hand; it might be time to separate from your company. Remember, as long as you are part of a company, you are a representative of that company. Like it or not, as I have mentioned before, it is not "You Inc."

You do have to trade some of your personal values for those of the company, for it is important to align with the company's culture.

This does not mean that you turn into something you are not. It does mean that you support the company in the culture that it is trying to build, even if some of its elements don't align with your own personal values.

For example, let's say you don't believe that being gay is a choice, or that you don't agree with the lifestyle. Don't focus on either of those issues. Focus on the idea that in the workplace, that gay person should be treated with respect and dignity and be given all the opportunities afforded to equally talented individuals. Use that same thinking as you look at other minority groups and related issues.

Cultural progress within a company means that you build upon the good attributes of the culture that the company already has. It means that you move it to be more inclusive in its practices and policies. You don't move it to a less-inclusive position. Focus on the attributes of the culture that needs to change. If you fundamentally believe that the company's culture does not have any positive attributes, you might want to reconsider your choice of company. Remember, take the company along with you—don't take the company on.

When you reframe your thinking along the lines of making progress, you start to see why it is important to bring every aspect of yourself to the table so that you can fully enable progress. In the process, involve everyone who can make the company more competitive and more successful in the markets it serves.

The Situation

Sid has been with Carthage Industries for a little over seven years. He is considered by management to be a real go-getter. He is always the first to offer up new ways of doing things, and he consistently delivers results in all his assignments. Sid has received accolades for his great work, not only inside the company but in the broader business community as well. He is a member of the Black Employees Resource Group (ERG) at his company and has been active in its journey. He sees where the company has made progress in the representation of blacks in the management ranks, and he is excited about that.

Sid is also gay, and he is less thrilled about the progress the company is making on gay issues. Although gays are included in the company's EEO policy, Sid feels that the company should also offer domestic partner benefits. He feels very strongly about this and is considering how he should broach the issue with the company. However, he has heard that some of the company's senior executives are homophobic, so he is unsure how to approach management with his concerns. He does not want to risk being looked at differently, any more than he already may be, and he does not want speaking out to negatively affect his standing within the company.

The Challenge

The challenge is: How patient should an employee be when observing progress in one area but not another? To look at this another way, how long does it take for a company's lack of progress to be perceived by that employee as a lack of desire by management to make the change? And then how long does it take to have a situation like this translate into a lack of engagement by that same employee?

Options and Probable Outcomes

Option 1: Sid continues to wait in silence, hoping that the LGBT ERG will approach management to make a change.

He voices his opinion to the LGBT ERG, hoping that it will take up the banner and approach management for domestic partner benefits.

The probable outcome is that it may or may not happen, depending upon the reputation and impact that the LGBT ERG has within the company. It is also possible that other people just like Sid are waiting for a group solution to avoid having to speak out individually.

Option 2: Sid sends and e-mail to several company leaders, conveying his dissatisfaction.

He makes it clear that more progress needs to be made in advancing LGBT benefits and indicates that he feels discriminated against.

The probable outcome is that Sid will alienate himself and will not be perceived as having the company's best interest at heart. Progress on the domestic partner benefits issue may even take a step back. Although Sid is a valuable contributor to the company, this approach may adversely impact his reputation in other ways.

Option 3: Sid works with the LGBT ERG to build a business case for why the company should offer domestic partner benefits.

He helps to articulate how it will benefit the company through employer branding and also from a competitive standpoint. In addition, Sid approaches his boss to ask for support. Working with the LGBT ERG members, he approaches other key executives and managers to ask for support. In these discussions, he leverages the business case.

The probable outcome is that domestic partner benefits may or may not be offered, but at least there is a foundation to build from in the future. Sid will have demonstrated his ability to be of influence outside his normal job, and he will also have demonstrated that he is looking out for both the company and himself.

Self-Improvement Tips

For the Individual

If your company offers ERGs, consider getting involved in the activity that both holds your interest and most benefits the company. Be willing to speak with management regarding improvement ideas. Learn to build a business case and a network of support.

What Can a Manager Do?

Practice being appropriately patient with the progress made at your company and/or in your specific organization/team. However, be very impatient when it comes to no progress. *Appropriate* in this context means that you see forward movement that is aligned with a reasonable timeline.

The Manager as Mentor

Always be open to employees from all areas of diversity. Be open to seeing ideas that come your way from a company value perspective. Offer to help make connections. If you cannot buy in to the idea/proposal being suggested, just say so, and then offer to connect the employee with someone who can help.

Situation Summary

Patience has never been my strong suit. However, as it relates to making progress on diversity and inclusive workplace practices, it is a necessary skill. This does not mean that you should sit around waiting for something to happen; it means that you should continue pressing forward to make progress by trying new approaches to address troubling areas, all the while being mindful that you cannot force fit. Diversity and inclusion work is not easy, but it is very rewarding. It's an area where you have to enjoy the journey, as well as the destination.

*Be the person you need to be, not the person
you think others want you to be.*

—Steven W. Lyle
Author

About the Author

Steve was born in Seneca, South Carolina in 1957. The youngest of five children, at the age of 5 Steve moved with his mother and father to Kentucky so that his father could find work. His parents were both blue collar workers with his mother always stressing, to all her children, the importance of education and striving to be more than people expect. Having lost his father at an early age and at the same time realizing at an early age that he was different created a lifelong journey to find and face the truth while striving to exceed people's expectations.

Steve has achieved success in the military, academia and in corporate America earning him top leadership roles and honors along.

He is currently the Chief Diversity Officer for Texas Instruments (TI) and a US Army Bronze star recipient. A father of two sons, he resides with his partner Daniel Thomas Kamide in Plano, Texas.